Juliet Roberts

OUTDOOR INTERIORS

Lannoo

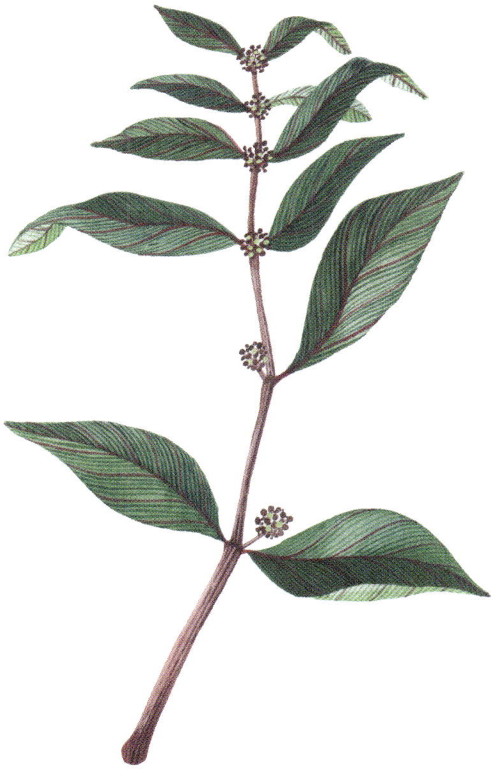

INTRODUCTION

WHAT MAKES A GREAT OUTDOOR SPACE?

Essentially, it's one that is a joy to use from a practical point of view and is a delight to look at. You'll know that it's a success simply by the fact that you spend increasing amounts of time enjoying it with friends, family or just by yourself.

But how do you get to this point? Firstly, I'd suggest looking with fresh eyes at the space you currently have and begin to think of it as an extension of your interior and very much a part of your home. As such, aim to create similar comforts to those indoors, for example cosy places to sit, cook, eat, lounge around and sleep. Consider how to get the best use from what you have available and the sort of 'look', 'feel' and 'emotional response' you'd like to have. With regards to aesthetics, there is no right or wrong as this will depend on your own personal taste, which, like you, is unique.

During the pandemic, many people realised the huge benefits of extending their homes into the outdoors. Properties with well-designed outdoor living areas have become more desirable than ever, so money spent on improvements is a good investment. It's worth bearing in mind that a beautiful outdoor space can improve the interior space too by offering a great view, a feeling of spaciousness and an engagement with the natural world.

It may be that you're starting with a blank canvas, or perhaps you've inherited something that needs refurbishing. This book is intended to help you by providing lots of visual inspiration of exceptional places from around the globe: outdoor spaces in which you can relax, enjoy yourself, entertain and have fun. The book also offers some insights into the design process, how to get the most out of your space, as well as key questions to ask (either yourself or a professional) and some important dos and don'ts.

STARTING

POINTS

WHATEVER SPACE YOU HAVE, it's possible to make it more joyful and user-friendly, but it does take some thought and astute planning. Time is an important factor too, as often our first ideas are not the best, and it's better to reflect on things and refine your ideas before making any serious investments.

Making plans

Creating a beautiful and useful outdoor area is not that dissimilar to designing the rooms inside your house, and the way in which you arrange the various elements as well as your choice of materials, colours and style will all impact the overall effect. Be aware of the things you choose to include or exclude and make sure that they are aesthetically pleasing and a joy to use. If they are meaningful in some way to you or your family, then this will help imbue your home with character and charm. Aim to create an outdoor oasis that you can escape to, where you can feel the sun on your face, listen to the birds sing, gaze at the night sky and have fun cooking, eating and spending time with family and friends.

Essentially, there are two ways of creating your ideal outdoor space: you can employ a professional designer or landscape architect, or you can do the work yourself. In either case, it's good to get a thorough understanding of your site, to plan carefully what you want from the design and consider the overall aesthetic. Everyone has their own agenda, so make sure you know what yours is and can articulate it clearly to those you might employ. Importantly, look at your budget and work out the maximum amount you wish to spend.

Understanding the site

Before attempting to figure out a design, spend time in your outdoor space at different times of the year, and at different times of the day, as this will help you assess the site in detail and understand what may or may not work. Leading garden designers and landscape architects suggest observing a garden over the course of a year to see what happens in each of the seasons. If you have the luxury of time then it is a great way of developing your thoughts on the best use of space. Potentially, it will also help you to avoid any big mistakes, thus saving you time, energy and money in the long run.

If you're renovating an existing outdoor area, a good first step is to take out as much as you can. Clear away any furniture, containers, clutter and unwanted plants. You may want to use this as an opportunity to give everything a good clean. Having a blank canvas makes it far easier to see how much space is available and what you have to work with.

Ask yourself are there any key elements, such as large trees, structures, driveways or services, that would be difficult or expensive to move? Are there any level changes that need to be taken into account? Where does excess rainwater go?

Orientation

The orientation of your garden is an important factor when planning your layout, so work out how the sun moves around the site and the effect this has at different times of the day and different times of the year. As a rule of thumb, in the northern hemisphere, the areas that face south will get the most sunshine and will become the hottest; whereas those facing north will receive the least light so will be cooler, darker and sometimes damper.

Take note of any tall trees or buildings close by and if so where the shadows fall. Sometimes heat can get reflected or trapped, or you'll find 'frost pockets' that become substantially colder than others. Find out which areas tend to retain the heat, and which cool down the quickest. Ask yourself: are some places affected by cold winds blowing through? How near are your neighbours? Are there roads close by? All these questions will help you decide the best approach.

View

The most beautiful spaces are often those that sit comfortably in their environment, in harmony with the wider setting. This is often achieved through hard landscaping materials, construction methods and detailing, in combination with the style, textures and colours of the furniture and soft furnishings.

Climate

In terms of climatic conditions, you can research the average rainfall in your area, and maximum and minimum temperatures. It's also good to take notice of air temperatures and the direction of the prevailing wind. Obviously, you may be able to mitigate against some of these to a greater or lesser extent. For instance, you can install structural elements, fencing or plant trees, shrubs or hedging to baffle the wind or provide shade. Nevertheless, it's always best to find ways you can work with the elements in the first instance.

Ideal spot

Invariably, some parts of the garden are more comfortable to be in at certain times of day than others, either because of the light, the shade, the view, because they're sheltered or somehow feel more private or magical. You'll often find that there is a perfect spot for a peaceful morning coffee and another for evening drinks. Sometimes it's difficult to fully explain why, but trust your instinct and be mindful of what feels good. It's well worth finding the locations that you'll be happiest in when eating, cooking, snoozing or whatever, because then you're more likely to use and enjoy them.

Sounds

A sense of privacy is important and while there are various ways you can create this, there may be areas of the garden that lend themselves more readily to this than others. This is not only in terms of being overlooked by neighbours but also the volume of sounds that you are exposed to. Take time to listen to the noises at different times of day. It's easy to underestimate the impact they can have on your enjoyment and certain areas may be affected more than others. The sounds may be something that you'd like to listen to – such as bird song or the rustling of plants in a breeze – or it may be something you'd prefer to avoid, for instance the sound of traffic, the neighbour's noisy children or dogs barking.

Locality

What is the wider setting like? Consider the vernacular architecture, local materials and the surrounding landscape. It can be interesting to research and find out what the traditional building materials and techniques are in your area. Often these come about because of geological or historic reasons linked to the practicalities and costs of moving materials from one location to another. Being aware of your surroundings – either through research, simply looking around you or talking to those who have local knowledge – will help develop your ideas. If possible, try and make a connection to the site through your hard landscaping elements, styles of construction and colours, etc., as it is these connections, however subtle, that will help to make your outside space sit more comfortably in the locale and therefore have a greater sense of place.

Plants

If you would like to include plants in your design, then I'd recommend assessing the quality of the soil. You can buy a little kit to find out the pH level; it also helps to pick it up, feel it and smell it. Does it contain lots of clay and retain moisture readily or it is sandy and free draining? Do you need to improve it before planting? Are there issues with perennial weeds? Check how deep the soil is and whether the conditions are generally damp or dry. All these factors, combined with the local weather conditions, will affect the type of plants that you can grow.

Bear in mind that your choice of plants can have a strong bearing on the overall atmosphere of your garden. Trees and shrubs can provide year-round structure; hedging can help bring a sense of privacy, mitigate against wind and muffle sounds, while perennials, bulbs and other more ephemeral seasonal planting can bring colour, texture, movement and special moments to look forward to as the seasons unfold. Plants, either in the ground or in pots, are a great way of changing an atmosphere, providing interest and lifting one's spirits.

Consider maintenance issues too and be realistic about how much time you have available to water, weed and look after plants as well as your skill as a gardener. It's easy to be seduced by dreamy pictures of beautiful planting schemes, but they often require ongoing care to thrive.

Purpose

Work out what exactly you want from the space and how it might fulfil its purpose. Bear in mind that the primary focus of your design should be about people, so work out who will use it. Will it be adults, seniors, children, teenagers? What is the age range of the main users? How physically active are you and those who will use the space? It is best to avoid lots of steps and level changes or areas that are difficult to navigate. Does it need to have wheelchair access? How many people will use it at any given time? When will they use it: will it be at certain times of the day or during evenings only? Is the intended use throughout the week or simply at the weekends? Is the outdoor space at a holiday home used only for a few weeks in summer? Do you need to include storage, heating, lighting? Importantly, what will people use it for? Will it be for eating and cooking? Is it for entertaining friends and family? Perhaps you might want to entertain business clients. Would it be a good idea to have several zones for different activities? If there will be multiple generations there, you may want to consider having a children's play area set apart from the adult dining area. Would you prefer to create an area for moments of peace and quiet, or perhaps for exercise?

There are myriad questions you can ask yourself and it's often worth sitting down with those who will use the space to discover what their specific wants and needs are. You may even be surprised! Draw up a list and take your time to think through the various permutations. Be mindful that we can all be guilty of dreaming about the life we think we should lead, which can be quite different to the one we have in reality. For instance, you may daydream about hosting elaborate barbecues for all your friends but in truth, will you? So be realistic about how the space will be used, when and by whom.

Work out how you can benefit from your outdoor space on a more day-to-day, week-by-week basis. Some things may see really obvious but write them down nevertheless. What you should aim for is a long list that covers all the possibilities as this can be reduced to just the essentials if need be. To be blunt, if the outdoor space doesn't meet the needs of those who actually use it, then you've missed an opportunity and to a large extent the design has failed. The most successful places – be they indoors or out – are those that are well used and well loved.

Once you've worked out the various areas/elements that you'd like to include in your outdoor space, next I'd recommend taking accurate measurements and making a scale drawing. Depending on the complexity of the site, this may be something you want to do yourself or you may prefer to commission someone else, such as a garden or landscape designer or landscaping contractor, to do this for you. A scale drawing is a great way of helping to focus one's attention on what may or may not be possible. Make sure to include any existing features that you wish or are obliged to retain as well as amenities such as electrics, water/drainage, septic tanks, etc. A drawing will help you to start building a picture of proportions, scale, necessary works and also get a handle on potential costs from the outset. There's nothing quite like seeing how a design works on the ground, so don't be afraid to mark things out with string and pins or line marker spray paint.

Zones

One of the best ways to organise your outdoor space, is to divide it into different areas for different activities. It not only makes it more dynamic but also can make it appear bigger. These distinct zones, often include spaces for dining, lounging, bathing, cooking and play. If you have children or grandchildren, it's a nice way of giving them space to feel free to play with their toys without the whole area becoming cluttered.

Landscape designers will often treat the zones as outdoor 'rooms' and emphasise their separateness by some form of divider such as hedging, tall plants, walls, archways, screens, buildings or climbing plants. Changes in level are also a good way of signalling that you are in a different space. The use of colour can make your zones feel distinct too, for instance having neutral tones for a calming effect and bright colours for more playful areas.

Creating 'rooms' also allows you to create mystery and intrigue with some areas partially hidden from view or completely secreted away. Moving from one area to the next can become like a journey, especially if each has a distinct purpose and personality.

Aesthetics

You can use a host of different things, including materials, colours, planting, furniture, soft furnishings and lighting to convey your particular style and a unique sense of place. Every element will play its part, as will the way in which they are positioned so bear in mind that it's how things are combined together that creates the overall effect. Rather than focusing on specific items, begin by working out how you want the area or individual zones to make you feel. Our 'reading' of a space depends on our emotional response to it. Would you like to create a calm, meditative atmosphere, or one that is lively and fun? How will the space complement what already exists? To get a cohesive sense of place, avoid buying things ad hoc and instead think about what you need and how it will fit into the overall scheme.

I'd highly recommend putting together a mood board of your ideas. To do this, just copy or cut out pages from magazines or print images found on the internet of items, colours, materials and outdoor spaces that particularly appeal to you. Group these together to see how the various things might work en masse, then edit by taking or adding other things until you're happy. You can also use sites such as Pinterest to find and collate ideas, inspiration and products. Mood boards are a useful way of seeing how things combine together and to work out what you/your family prefer before going ahead and making any purchases. Think of it as 'tantric shopping'!

Bear in mind that it's not just the 'things' that you plan to buy that will affect the overall look, but also what already exists on site – such as paving, stonework, buildings and structures, lighting, boundaries and fencing – so it's worth including images of those too. Aim for a limited number of materials and a finely tuned palette of colours.

ELEMENTS OF STYLE

THERE ARE NUMEROUS ELEMENTS

that need to be considered for the purposes of creating a practical and stylish outdoor space. While the list below is not comprehensive, I have included the most important constituent parts that will help you make it beautiful and a joy to spend time in.

BOUNDARIES

The boundaries of your outdoor space play an important role in the overall aesthetic as well as the peace and comfort of time spent outdoors. Boundaries are often installed for security reasons or for defining the edges of your property, but they are also useful for creating a sense of privacy, to screen off the neighbours or unwanted views, and to improve the overall aesthetic.

The best boundaries are the ones that blur into their surroundings by appearing to merge with what's beyond. It's worth being aware that the smaller the garden is, the more important it is to disguise walls as they are closer and therefore have a more dominant presence than in a larger garden.

Hedging & climbing plants

The most straightforward way to achieve this is by using hedging plants to form a barrier, however, if this is not possible and you have to have fencing then it's well worth using climbing plants to make it 'disappear'.

Hedges make a wonderful backdrop, are excellent at filtering the wind, and create safe havens and a source of food for wildlife. With both hedging and climbing plants, it is important to take into consideration whether or not the plant is evergreen, scented, the speed at which it grows and how much maintenance it requires.

The benefit of evergreen plants is that you get year-round cover. However, you may prefer to have that plants lose their leaves over autumn and winter and allow more light into the area during those darker months. The speed of growth and the amount of maintenance is also important. Remember, if you want plants to grow quickly to create a hedge or cover a wall then they are not just going to stop when they've done so! If you'd prefer to reduce the amount of pruning and cutting back, it may be better to be patient and choose something that grows slowly. Be aware that some of the more vigorous climbers can potentially damage walls and fences once established, so you may want to consider installing a separate frame or a strong system of wire supports for them to grow up.

Fencing

The most popular material for boundaries is wooden fencing as it sits well in the landscape, comes in numerous styles, is relatively long-lasting and often cheaper than other options. To ensure wooden fences have as long a lifespan as long as possible, it is best to choose either a softwood such as pine that has been treated with a wood preservative (often referred to as 'tanalised' wood) or, if your budget allows, then a good quality hardwood. In terms of style, it's worth looking around to see what is used locally. If you live in the countryside, a more rustic look might work best, whereas if you live in a city then something smarter and more 'finished' is often preferable. You can also buy metal fencing such as railings, estate fencing or chain-link.

The height of your fence is also an important consideration and it's advisable to check local planning laws to find out what is permissible. In general terms, fences of around 1.8m provide a decent amount of privacy without feeling too dominant. Bear in mind the taller your fence, the more light you will block out. Solid fencing can cause the wind to eddy, damaging plants and sometimes causing fences to fall over, therefore those that have gaps or are woven and allow some degree of wind to blow through them work best in windy situations.

In terms of security, interestingly, a wobbly rickety fence can be more of an impediment than a strong one that is easy to climb over.

As for the uprights, they are generally softwood, hardwood or concrete posts, all of which will need to be sunk into holes in the ground. While wooden posts often look better and more in keeping with the fence material, they will need replacing far sooner than concrete. You can generally expect them to last around 10 to 25 years. If your fence is painted, I'd suggest painting the concrete posts in the same colour as a way of making them less obvious. Always check the boundary line of your property before putting in your fence as you shouldn't assume that any existing fences have been installed in the correct place. It's also a good idea to discuss your plans with your neighbours as you may need to have access from their side when putting up the fence.

For construction, use stainless steel screws. For a smarter look, you can recess the screw and hide the top with wooden dowels. If painting or staining the wood, use a product suitable for outdoor use and bear in mind that darker colours recede, and brighter, lighter colours appear to come forward.

PATIOS & VERANDAS

Areas where you plan to sit or dine benefit from a hard-wearing, easy-to-clean surface. If you'd like protection from the sun, wind and rain then you may also want to consider some form of overhead cover.

These days the words 'patio' and 'terrace' are used interchangeably. Some think the word patio a bit downmarket, however, essentially patio and terrace mean exactly the same: a level area, either paved or with some form of flat, hard surface, that can be used for seating or dining. Generally, they adjoin the house or a building and are often the main point of transitions from the interior to the exterior space. A deck is a timber platform that is generally attached to a building. Terraces play an important role in outdoor living, often being the most frequently used of all the outdoor spaces and, as such, can contribute enormously to the quality of time spent relaxing, eating and entertaining alfresco.

Verandas and porches play a similar role to the above but invariably have a roof attached to the outside of the house and are often partially enclosed by railings to the front and sides. Porches are used in front of the entrance to a building and tend to be smaller than verandas, which will generally extend along most of the width of the building.

As well as being positioned adjacent to the house, terraces and verandas can be set apart and used as a destination point for dining, cooking or alongside a swimming pool.

Before building any permanent structure, check if you need planning permission and any building regulations. It's not just the size and location but also the height that can be an issue. Do your research and get permissions in advance, as there's no point in having great ideas if you can't put them into effect.

Use

Once that is clarified, give some thought to what you want to use the area for, and the shape and dimensions that will best suit its purpose. How often will you use the space? How many people do you need to accommodate? Do you want to eat, cook and entertain there? If you want to eat out regularly and don't wish to have cooking facilities, don't locate the patio too far from your kitchen as it will become a bore to-ing and fro-ing between the two. Often, terraces have to fulfil multiple purposes including dining, relaxing, entertaining and children's play areas. Broadly speaking, strong simple shapes work best visually, are easier to install and are more cost effective than complex shapes.

In terms of size, the area should be in proportion to the house or adjacent buildings and comfortable to use. If it's too small, things can feel pinched, and be awkward or even dangerous to navigate. Ideally, the terrace should create a relationship between the architecture, any nearby garden areas and the wider landscape, as it is often the first step you make on a journey from interior to the exterior world.

It's worth thinking about the size and style of the furniture you plan to use in the space as this can also affect how the proportions work. Are there level changes that will require steps or slopes? Where are these best located? Dining areas are particularly important to get right. A common mistake is to design them with the seats tucked beneath the table whereas in fact it important to make sure that there is plenty of space to pull out the dining chairs without risking toppling over the edge of a terrace. If in doubt about the size of your terrace, it's invariably better to go larger.

Location

Ideally your terrace will be located in a convenient, tranquil spot that's relatively flat and maximises any view. Bear in mind that people tend to be lazy and the more convenient the location, the better the chance that it will become well loved and well used.

If you decide to have the terrace as a destination, make doubly sure that there is a really good reason to head out there. Remember on hot days, people will seek out the coolest spot to relax and hardly anyone can resist flames, so you may want to think along the lines of including a pizza oven, barbecue area or fire pit.

Another practicality is rainwater run-off. Large, hard surfaces should be built in such a way that they slope away from any adjacent buildings. Depending on the size and location of your terrace, you may need to consider some form or drainage system.

Materials

Hard outdoor surfaces for terraces and patios can be made from various things, including brick, stone, slabs, pebble mosaics, unglazed tiles, wood, composite materials or concrete. For areas set apart from the house you could also consider hoggin (a mix of sand, gravel and clay that compacts to a stable surface) or crushed rock. Ideally, you should avoid loose material such as gravel, as it moves too much underfoot and, particularly if the terrace is near the house, has a tendency to make its way indoors.

Think about the size and shape of the units of material you intend to use. Smaller units, particularly if the grouting between them is large, can appear busy, and they are also more expensive to lay. Larger paving set tightly together can appear calmer. The direction that you lay paving can make your patio look wider or narrower: if rectangular-shaped paving is laid lengthways away from the house it has the effect of drawing the eye out and making the area appear longer and narrower; conversely if set lengthways along the house then it will make it seems shorter and wider.

Whatever material you choose, the most important thing is that the surface is hard-wearing and easy to clean. It should also be even and stable, as you want to avoid creating any trip hazards.

Designers will often use the same flooring material used in the house to extend outdoors. This gives a more seamless look, makes a lovely connection between the two spaces and can make both appear larger than they actually are.

Although you will no doubt use the terrace or veranda predominantly in summer, it's worth thinking about how it will look in winter too. You may not necessarily be sitting out there, but if you have views of it from the house then it's worth making sure it's as attractive as possible during any downtime. In autumn, I'd suggest having a good tidy up, storing away as much as you can, then hanging up fairy lights or festoon lighting across the space. Grey winter days are always improved with a bit of sparkle!

PATHS & WALKWAYS

The design, materials and shape of your paths have an important bearing on the aesthetics as well as the practicalities of navigating your way around. It should go without saying that a path needs a destination. Paths can be used on a purely practical level to connect different areas together or to provide access or guide the eye towards something; conversely, it can be employed as a diversionary tactic to guide our gaze away from something unattractive.

As for the shape, the main options are between a straight path that takes you the quickest route from A to B, or a curved or snaking design that lends itself to a slower, more meandering pace. Straight paths tend to appear formal, while curved paths often lend a more casual, relaxed feel. The width of the path also has a bearing on how it looks and how it can be used. From a design perspective you can use a long, skinny path to accentuate the narrowness of a garden or paths that run from side to side to make the space feed wider.

The texture and colour of the surface material will affect how it looks and feels underfoot. Make sure that it looks good and is also fit for purpose. Do you want a hard surface to tie in with your terrace or would loose gravel suffice? Ideally, choose a material that will blend with the other elements already in place, including the architecture of the house, terraces, garden walls, etc. Think about where the pathway will be located. Perhaps it is beneath trees or in a damp area of the garden that could become slippery, in which case it's best to have a textured surface. As with terraces, there are numerous options for materials and obviously prices vary enormously.

OUTDOOR KITCHENS

For some reason there's something wonderfully primal and profoundly fulfilling about cooking and eating outdoors. Maybe it connects us to early man (or most likely early woman), and the simplicity of time spent outdoors with family and friends preparing, cooking and eating together.

In light of the pandemic, more people now prefer to entertain outside and building an outdoor kitchen-cum-dining area is arguably one of the best home improvements you can make.

Whether you opt for a highly sophisticated outdoor kitchen with all the bells and whistles or a simple charcoal grill, there are lots of options and your choice will depend on your budget, lifestyle, what you like to cook, the size and layout of the space available as well as your sense of aesthetic. Work out what's essential and what would make you happy. Cooking and eating outside doesn't need to be overly complicated for it to be fun.

Importantly, make sure that your outdoor kitchen is safe. During the summer months, we are generally more scantily clad and it's easier to get burns from hot oil splashes and boiling liquids such as sauces. Allow plenty of space around cooking facilities for ease of movement; it's also vital that there are no trip hazards so avoid using outdoor rugs or positioning outdoor kitchens close to steps. Keep pets, young children and their toys at bay. It's also wise to have a decent first-aid kit within easy reach, particularly if your outdoor cooking area is at a distance from the house.

FURNITURE

Just as with your interiors, it makes a huge difference to your enjoyment of a space if you have somewhere convenient to perch, sit, lounge around or even sleep. And there's no reason why you can't have the same comforts outdoors as you do indoors.

Firstly, consider your budget and think about whether you want to invest in quality furniture that is likely to stand the test of time, or if you just want a quick fix with something cheap and cheerful. Before buying, make sure you have considered exactly what you need for the space and how the various things might fulfil their purpose. Bear in mind that gardens are more relaxed, informal spaces, so be as generous as you can when spacing your seating.

Check the size of the furniture and make sure that when put together as a collection, everything fits to scale. Dinky little chairs on a huge terrace can look disproportionate and silly; conversely vast loungers in a limited space can make the area awkward and annoying to navigate. Try not to underwhelm or overwhelm the space.

If in doubt about whether the furniture will fit in the given space, mark out the sizes where they will be used, making sure you have enough space for them to function well. It is all too easy to be seduced by furniture on the internet or glossy magazines, but there is nothing quite like testing things out in person for comfort, the quality of the materials and how well they are actually made.

General tips for buying furniture: make sure it is comfortable, well built, of suitable materials for outdoor use and hard-wearing. If items include fabric, cushions or bolsters, check they are waterproof and fade resistant.

Instead of buying off-the-peg items or second hand, you may want to create something bespoke. Whatever you opt for, it's important that the furniture feels as if it's an intrinsic part of the design aesthetic. A cohesive approach to colours, materials and textures always helps to tie everything together.

LIGHTING

Lighting has the ability to radically alter the atmosphere of your outdoor space. It can make time spent outdoors far more enjoyable and allow you to spend longer al fresco in comfort. It is also invaluable on a purely practical level too, as a way of increasing visibility on paths, steps and entrances. Another important consideration is security and making sure that lighting automatically switches on in key areas to deter intruders. Whatever its purpose, to get the best out of any lighting scheme, you need to consider positioning, intensity, colour and style. In essence, you can use many of the same principles for lighting an outdoor space as you would inside your home. Layering and flexibility are key.

Bear in mind that the bulb wattage you use indoors will look considerably different outside lighting up the dark. A common mistake is to use a bulb with a higher wattage than is necessary. Most outdoor fixtures will be rated for either wet locations or damp locations. Those 'wet rated' are designed for situations exposed directly to rain; whereas 'damp rated' are suited to outdoor covered areas.

If possible, it is wise to install lighting systems at the time your outdoor space is being built as this makes it easier to get electrical points where you need them most and wiring can be neatly hidden away. Make sure that the lighting you choose is fit for use outdoors and always use a qualified electrician for installations.

HEATING

Finding ways to stay cosy outside as temperatures drop means you can extend the time you enjoy your outdoor space – but what's the best choice? The unavoidable truth is that from an environmental point of view, heating the outside air is a no-no. It's also inefficient and expensive. That said, there are undoubtedly numerous physical and mental health benefits to spending time outdoors. If you feel you need some form of heating, then at least it's good to weigh up the pros and cons as well as the ecological impact of various options. Most common are a patio heater, a fire pit and chiminea. In terms of carbon footprint, whether you use propane, natural gas, electricity or wood will depend on a number of factors, not least where you live.

To alleviate any feelings of guilt, you could consider turning off your indoor heating when you are using heating outdoors or make other sacrifices, such as taking the train rather than flying, as a way of reducing your overall energy consumption and emissions output. The only other option is to wear warm outdoor clothing, including silk or merino base layer, alpaca socks and warm hat and gloves as these can really help counter chilly weather. You could also invest in a thermal camping blanket or sleeping bag to keep cosy.

SHADE

As much as many of us love sunshine, there are times when we want to be outdoors in the cool shade or want to protect ourselves from excess UV rays. There are a number of ways of creating shade in your garden, including using particular plants, building a pergola to sit beneath, extending the house with a veranda, installing awnings, rigging up a shade sail or simply using parasols.

Depending on whereabouts in the world you live and how much time you want to spend outdoors, it's worth considering whether you need to create deep shade, part shade or just light, dappled shade. Also, think about how shade may affect any planting, and if you use something that will create permanent shade, what the impact this may have during autumn or winter. Even though you may want to block out bright sunshine in the summer, you may not want the same space to be dark and dingy out of season.

FOCAL POINTS

Ornamental features, such as sculptures, urns, fountains or even planting, are a good way to inject interest, personality and distinctiveness into your outdoor space. Some practical items, including firepits, ponds, benches or water, can also be used for a similar effect.

Focal points are a good way of guiding one's gaze either towards a certain view or something of interest or, conversely, away from things you'd prefer not to draw attention to, either in your own space or in the wider setting.

To catch the viewer's eye and sustain their attention, it is better to keep focal points simple. If you have too many objects, it can be distracting and counterproductive as the eye will wander. Better to choose a few items that you really love and position them to best advantage. As with the natural landscape, it's good for the eye to look into the distance as well as have interest in the middle ground and closer up. And it's not just visuals: the sound of splashing or flowing water, bird song and the scent of flowers, especially roses, can become points of interest.

GET THE LOOK

WHATEVER STYLE GARDEN YOU WANT to create, think about how you want it to make you feel. Our emotional response to a space – whether it's a feeling of calm, joy, playfulness or peace – will greatly affect how much you end up using the space. So consider the atmosphere you want to create before choosing any of the elements. Remember the overall look and feel of a space will be a sum of its parts. If a number of those parts don't fit the bill, then you will lose the main impact of what you want to achieve.

In this section you'll find some basic guidelines for how certain looks have been created, However, the way in which we perceive a space is often very personal. Please don't take these as strict guidelines, but rather as food for thought. As with many things in life, it's good to know the rules before deciding if you want to break them!

GET THE LOOK

TRADITIONAL

THE WORD 'TRADITIONAL' implies a conventional design that has stood the test of time, and that is also to a certain extent a bit old-fashioned. If you'd like to create a traditionally styled garden, then aim for a look that appears as if it has been settled in place for some time. The layout should be simple and understated; symmetry often works particularly well to create a balanced and comfortable atmosphere. As for hard landscaping materials, choose those that are time-honoured and will age well, such as stone, oak, brick and steel.

If you can find good quality reclaimed materials, such as paving, tiles, stonework, then all the better, as these will often already bear the patina of age. You may be surprised how the small, subtle details that come with time-worn materials can greatly add to the overall look. Think about the different effect imparted by new stone compared to old, to the patina of age found on old copper as opposed to a brand new one. A good tip used to speed up the ageing on terracotta pots, often used by designers or those creating show gardens, is to paint them with plain yoghurt. After about a month, the surface will have developed a natural-looking texture of moss and algae.

Vintage furniture can also add a huge amount of charm, however, if you can't find suitable original pieces there are plenty of fine quality new pieces available too. Again, look for honest materials, timeless design, good craftsmanship and proportions that work well in the setting.

Any structures, such as pergolas, arbours, verandas and covered terraces should ideally be made with classic proportions and of traditional materials. They often benefit from small details such as shaped columns, finials, latticework or some other form of ornamentation or sculptural feature to give them more character.

As for colours – for example painted wood or metal, soft furnishings, awnings, parasols – a relatively conservative, perhaps even old-fashioned range of colours works best, such as neutrals, black, dark greens, chocolate browns, blues, greys, deep reds and plum colours. Best avoid primary, garish or neon colours unless you're feeling very confident in the way you introduce them. Swimming pools, in particular, work better in a traditionally styled environment if you avoid the ubiquitous bright turquoise-blue and opt instead for more subtle colours such as grey blues, dark green or even black.

In terms of features around the garden, classic figurative sculptures and large vintage urns in stone, terracotta or metal work well. Simple fountains, brick or stone-edged pools and vintage or classic water bowls all suit a traditional set up.

Greenery is a good way to impart a timeless atmosphere, whether that's lawn, an elegant oak tree, yew hedging, roses climbing up supports or abundant flower beds, pots or containers.

There's something straightforward about traditional outdoor spaces and everything about them is intended to get better with age. So consider all of the elements that you choose to include and how they work together to create a picture of elegance, calm and comfort.

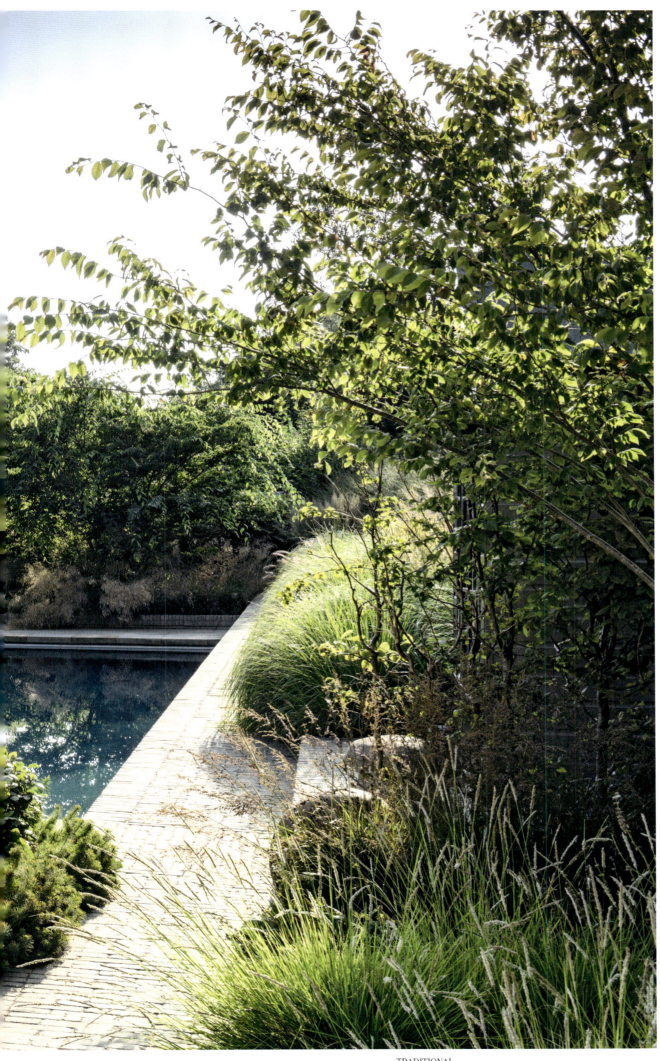

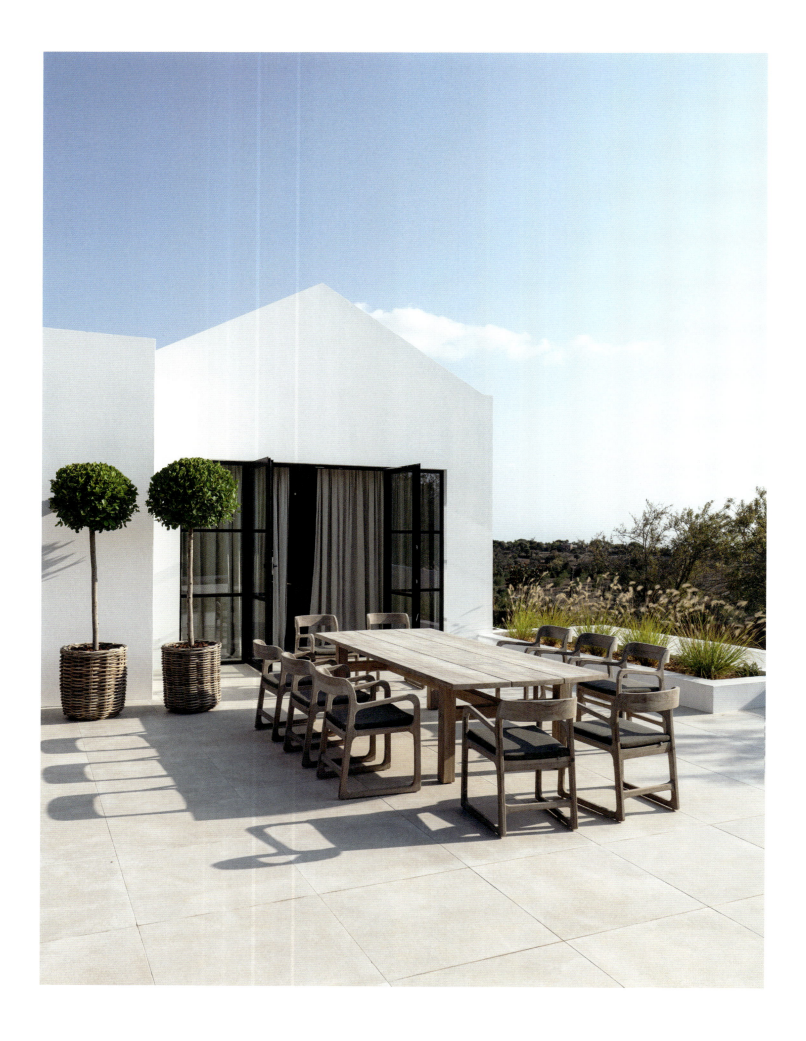

GET THE LOOK

GET THE LOOK

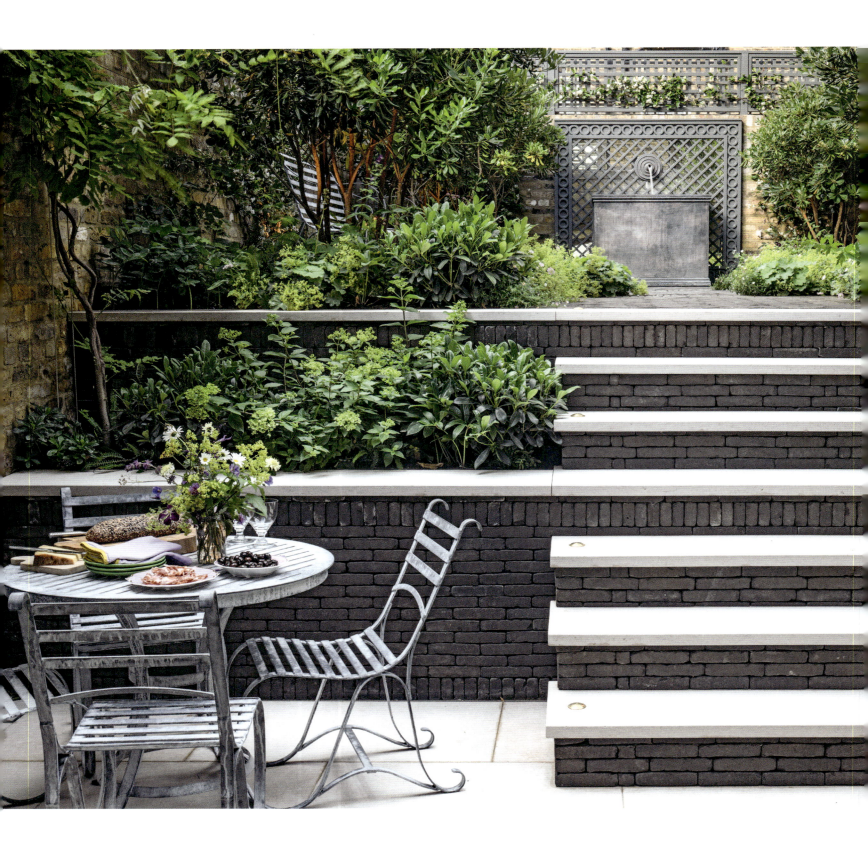

GET THE LOOK

GET THE LOOK

ROOM WITH A VIEW

Each element of this undercover dining area has been carefully considered to create a cosy, rustic elegance. Simple but effective, this space is a charming place to dine, come rain or shine.

1 The chimney breast is made of rough-hewn stone in grey and a warm buff with buff-coloured mortar joints. The lintel is formed from an arch of stone in a light natural colour, so it ties it all together. The combination of textures has a pleasingly rustic look. The chimney is of a substantial width so it has a strong presence; however, the simple design and neutral tones ensure that it doesn't overly dominate.

2 The fireplace is raised to around the eye-height of those sitting at the dining table to ensure they have a view of the flames. When not lit, the fire basket can be loaded up with logs to make a pleasing composition. A traditional, black cast-iron fire back sits beneath the fire basket as ornamentation and textural detail, with the colour tying it with the black metal of the fire basket. There's plenty of space in the area beneath the fire for loading up firewood, which not only looks attractive, but also makes it easy and less time-consuming to replenish the fire when in use.

3 Simple but elegant wooden chairs (and one may assume a matching table beneath the tablecloth) echo the wood used for the beams supporting the wooden roof. The use of wood ensures that the materials are kept to a limited palette and nothing jars. The slats of the chairs allow a certain amount of light in to brighten the table. Covered structures can often be gloomy places so ideally you should let in as much sunshine as possible.

4 A pale coloured climbing rose softens the stone wall and makes the whole seem more romantic from the start and, if scented, would softly perfume the air as guests walk in. It's worth noting that the structure supporting the roof is built of the same stone as the fireplace. The neutral colour of the limestone rendering on the walls matches that of the pointing between the bricks and add to a general sense of calm. In a subtle way, it also points to the attention to detail that has gone into the structure's design and build.

5 Beds of lavender spilling gently onto the paving close to the entrance would also add scent. They help soften the rectilinearity of the paving stones and lead the eye out to the planting in the wider landscape beyond. A note about lavender: it is an easy-to-grow shrub that likes free-draining soil in full sun. It is tolerant of drought and does not like the damp and cold. Many are hardy, but some are not – so worth checking what suits your location.

6 Trees form a lush green backdrop to the scene. They give a sense of enclosure and will mitigate against wind blowing into the dining area.

7 The visible wooden beams of the roof are a mix of old and new, however, new wood always silvers down with age and becomes less obviously 'new'.

8 The colour of the stone paving works extremely well with the stone-built walls and lime render. They are large, which means far fewer joints, so are easy on the eye. They are generous too, meaning visitors can stand outside the structure and enjoy the view and the planting before taking their place at the table.

WARM WELCOME

An attractive, comfortable seating area with a fireplace is always a huge draw. Maybe it's because it strongly echoes the components of an interior lounge or maybe it's the primordial connection with the importance of fire. The location of the outdoor seating is key: the ideal spot is out of the wind, with good light as well as shade during the hottest time of the day.

1. The relatively fine, buff-coloured gravel is easy to walk on and an economical way to cover large areas. It also lends itself well to plants growing up through it. It's advisable to lay a permeable, weed-resistant membrane down first to reduce weeds taking a hold (and the time spent clearing them!). Before putting down the gravel, cut out holes in the membrane where you wish to put any plants. For pathways, gravel should be laid at least 4-5cm deep.

2. Some trees, such as this eucalyptus, are grown in such a way that they have multiple stems (unsurprisingly you'll find them labelled as 'multi-stem'). They generally have a more sculptural presence than trees grown with a single trunk, so are great for adding interest and dynamism. The eucalyptus leaves, which have leathery green tops and silvery undersides, will also perfume the air with their cooling scent. Most types of eucalyptus do best in a warm, sunny location and when happy can grow vigorously into majestic trees. Fortunately, they are happy to be pruned hard to keep them to a compact shape.

3. The stone terrace sits slightly higher than the pathway surrounding it, which helps prevent the gravel being inadvertently kicked on to it. The colour of the stone matches that of the fireplace surround, and both coordinate well with the gravel. Although the chairs are large, and designed to be relatively static, there is plenty of space behind them to pull them out if need be.

4. The simply designed wooden furniture fits the space perfectly in terms of its proportions to the terrace, as well as being at the perfect height for those seated to enjoy the open fire. The colour of the plump upholstery matches the backdrop of the fire surround and has subtle dark, purple-coloured piping with back cushions to match. A generous, matching table has been placed between the easy chairs and is the perfect height for drinks.

5. The stone fire surround forms not only a home for the fire but also a feature wall to the whole seating area, giving the space a stronger sense of identity. The mix of pales stones in creams and greys reflect the light and coordinate perfectly with the paving, the gravel and even the upholstery. The large, blackened aperture for the fire gives a sense of depth too and is generous enough so that all of those seated can enjoy the flames.

6. The lower-level plantings of rosemary works well with the eucalyptus in terms of colour, texture and form. An aromatic, easy-going, drought-tolerant shrub, it is useful for providing ground cover around the trees and for lining the narrow pathway. It can be clipped into a mix of loose and clipped forms to add interest and texture. The benefit of having a predominance of green is that it helps bring about a restful atmosphere. Narrow pathways are a great way of slowing visitors down and encouraging them to better enjoy their time outdoors.

7. If used carefully, touches of colour, such as this coral-leaved plant and the purple cushions, can help enliven a collection of otherwise very muted tones.

INSIDE OUT

Comfortable seating with generous proportions, a large shady area, stone paving and a view out on to greenery all help make time spent outdoors during long hot summer days far more enjoyable. Natural materials and a muted colours add to the cool, relaxed atmosphere.

1 The wooden veranda, which extends out from the side of the house, offers protection from both sun and rain. The choice of wood for the uprights, beams and roof lining imparts a strong rustic feel that fits in well with the rural setting.

2 Woven blinds can be rolled down to mitigate strong sunshine and allow the area to be used comfortably for longer periods of time.

3 Generous seating such as these sofas, which wrap around a low coffee table, lends itself to relaxation, conversation and a feeling of togetherness. The neutral colours of the sofas and cushions underscore the veranda's calm, cool atmosphere.

4 The perimeter of the paved area is edged with low hedging. This not only makes a connection to the wider landscape but also provides a buffer against strong winds blowing into the covered space.

5 Simple glass lanterns containing candles are an elegant and cost-effective way of adding light and atmosphere during the evening.

6 Stone paving such as this is a great option for outdoor living areas as it looks great, wears well, is weather-resistant and easy to clean. Again the colours are natural and neutral and so are easy on the eye. Using a mix of different shaped stones adds subtle interest and fits in well with the overall rustic tone.

SHOP RESPONSIBLY

Buying materials and products that are produced or sourced sustainably and responsibly means that as consumers we can reduce our negative impact on the environment and improve the livelihood and working conditions of the producers. Environmental issues relating to construction could easily fill an entire book, the main point is that, given the climate crisis, it's in our own interest to be conscious of what we buy and create, and aim to do so as thoughtfully and sustainably as possible.

CONSIDER WHAT TO LEAVE OUT

Bear in mind that with any 'editing' process, what you decide not to include is just as important as what you do want to include. If you make sure that there is no clutter and a relationship between the various elements, then your outdoor space will automatically feel calmer and more considered.

GET THE LOOK

CONTEMPORARY

OUTDOOR SPACES styled in a contemporary manner suggest that they are very much of the moment, with the latest in design, materials and construction techniques. Creating something that isn't bound by convention, where pretty much anything goes, is incredibly liberating. There's joy too from being bang up to date with all the state-of-the-art gadgets, materials and methods. The slight downside to all of this is that anything super contemporary can easily date, so it's worth having that at the back of one's mind.

The best contemporary gardens tend to have bold layouts, a considered use of space and flawless execution. They often feature clean lines and bold geometric shapes and invariably there's a crisp finish to the hard landscaping elements and a distinct lack of ornamentation. However, there is no reason why your layout can't be sleek and curvaceous – the main thing is that the space should have a sculptural, unfussy aesthetic. Clean lines and a lack of ornamentation generally lend a space a certain calmness, however, contemporary spaces can be so 'cool' as to be slightly sterile. It doesn't take much to counter this. Simply adding textural details, spots of colour or unexpected pieces of sculpture can give a space a more human touch.

Arguably, contemporary styling lends itself more readily to the blurring of boundaries between outdoor and indoor spaces than, say, traditional styling where often there is more of a distinction. 'Outdoor' rooms that have a strong connection to the interior will always make the whole feel bigger and more expansive. Simple ways to achieve this include having the same material underfoot between the two areas and large floor-to-ceiling windows or doors that open out so that the two areas flow seamlessly together physically and aesthetically so as to feel almost as if they are one. Using a similar palette of materials, colours, furniture and soft furnishings can also help this feeling of connectedness.

Hard landscaping for contemporary space often includes materials such as concrete, wood, crisply cut stone, ceramic tiles, stainless and Corten steel. The overall finish is polished and sleek with great attention to detail. Paving is often made up of large units to reduce the fussiness of numerous joints and poured concrete, with its seamless finish is also very popular.

There's a wide range of outdoor modern furniture on the market, from sleek dining sets and sofas to chic daybeds and hanging chairs. Textiles and finishing are often state of the art and resistant to all sorts of weather conditions while still being comfortable and good-looking.

Structures in the garden are best kept simple and sleek, again with minimal ornamentation. Those that work best celebrate the nature of the material they are made from, such as metal pergolas with strong, slim supports, cantilevered roofs over dining areas and stepping stones that appear to float across the top of a pond. The latest techniques and clever engineering open up myriad possibilities for design and construction.

A wide range of colours work in a contemporary setting and are an easy way of creating a chic atmosphere. Whites, greys and neutrals feature heavily in contemporary designs; however, designers will often inject a shot of colour to create a less formal note.

As for focal points and features, it goes without saying that modern sculptural pieces work exceptionally well in these settings. However, these don't necessarily have to be things that look as if they have been computer generated; there are some spectacular contemporary designs by leading artisans and makers. Often when an artwork has a more handmade, tactile quality, it can create very interesting and dynamic compositions. Pots and containers are also a great way of bringing interest to a design, especially if they have a sculptural quality in their own right.

Contemporary styling tends to work better in urban spaces rather than countryside setting, however, much depends on the architecture of the house. Contemporary styling of outdoor spaces tends to focus more on the hard landscaping elements rather than the planting (sometimes referred to as 'soft scaping') so are well suited to those that prefer less garden maintenance. That said, there are also plenty of planting styles that work well with architecturally driven design, including ornamental grasses, bamboos, clipped evergreens and plants that typify the 'new perennial movement', whose more naturalistic look makes a dynamic juxtaposition.

GET THE LOOK

GET THE LOOK

GET THE LOOK

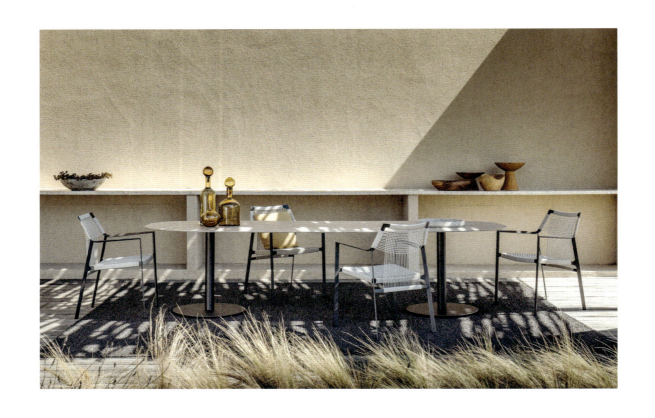

GET THE LOOK

GET THE LOOK

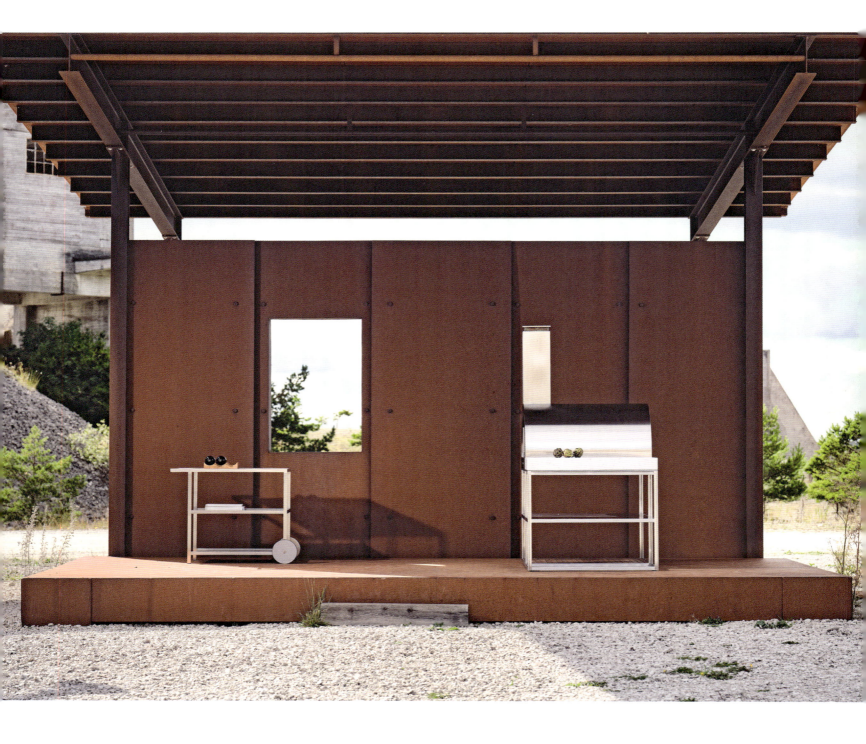

GET THE LOOK

SHELTERED SPOT

This modern take on a fire pit makes great use of the courtyard area between two new wooden buildings. While the space has a clear identity of its own, it sits beautifully with the architecture and, unusually, manages to appear both thoroughly modern and snug at the same time.

1 The silvered wooden decking brings lightness to the courtyard area, and the relatively narrow planks laid horizontally help make the area feel wider. Wood is a popular choice for decking as the natural material has a warmth and softness to it and sits well outdoors. Here it contrasts with the golden hues of the wood buildings and is easy on the eye as the planks run in the same direction as those used on the vertical plane.

2 Concrete is a popular material for contemporary spaces. It is strong, durable and versatile and has the added benefit of requiring minimal maintenance, so is ideal if your time is limited. Here it is shaped into a block that serves to break up the space and also functions as a simple bench or table. Note the discreet lighting tucked into the side of it, which would cleverly signal the drop in light at night.

3 Planting of hedging at the boundary line helps create a neutral lush green backdrop. These are clipped, which helps distinguish them from the looser natural planting in the wider landscape. Most hedging is relatively static so planting wispy grasses that rustle in the breeze brings sound and movement. Planting groups of grasses so that they guide the eye from the foreground near the house to the end of the pathway helps entice the visitor down the path to see what lies beyond.

4 The low square fire pit sits within a bigger square that functions both as seating and also as a walkway. The subtle change in colours in this seating area ensures the silver grey of the wood and concrete block don't predominate.

5 Gravel in a warm buff tone adds texture. Being relatively inexpensive it is perfect for larger areas, particularly if you want plants to break up large expanses of it. A small detail: the level of the gravel sits slightly lower than that of the pathway or seating area, which helps lessen gravel being kicked out of place.

6 The pathway extends the wooden decking and leads the eye to the far end of the garden. Long narrow paths such as this can give a slightly false sense of perspective and help trick the eye into thinking that the area is longer than it is in reality.

7 The simple, low-level seating and table continue the grey theme. However, being a few shades darker than the wooden decking and concrete, they help bring a certain connection to the grey details on the building behind as well as well as on the tops of the wooden pillars opposite.

GET THE LOOK

INTO
THE
WOODS

An elegant pool area that is sleek yet comfortable. The contemporary design of the pool and loungers work well together, yet it is the use of a refined colour palette and subtle textural elements that really set this design apart.

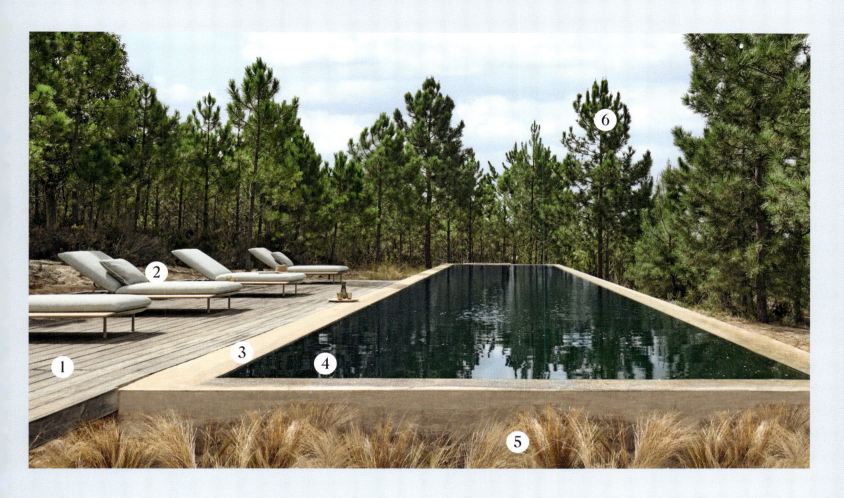

1. The area around a pool plays an important part in the overall aesthetic. Timber decking is a popular choice as it is non-slip and hard-wearing. It is important to choose a suitable hardwood timber as it needs to cope with water (often laden with chemicals) and the extremes of summer and winter weather.

2. The sleek, understated loungers add to the overall look of quiet elegance. The best pads and cushions have washable covers, which is important if fabrics are likely to regularly get damp.

3. The immediate edge around the top of a pool, known as coping, always plays a significant role. Concrete is a particularly good choice as it is hard-wearing, non-slip and can be tinted to match the other elements used in the design.

4. Rather than opt for the oft-seen bright blue pool liner, why not instead choose a more natural colour such as this dark blue green? Darker colours reflect the sky and surrounding vegetation far better than pale colours, and often give a space a greater degree of sophistication.

5. Low-level ornamental grasses tend to be low maintenance and if chosen well will provide summer and autumn interest with colour and texture. The tawny shades here are exceptionally well suited to the colour of the coping and timber deck.

6. A green backdrop, such as these tall pines, gives a sense of enclosure and restfulness. The juxtaposition of a contemporary space against a natural setting often emphasises their singular beauty.

IN THE SHADE

This sophisticated seating space sits beneath a modern take on the veranda. Neutral colours often produce an atmosphere of calmness but can appear somewhat bland, so the trick is to include textural elements, natural materials and plants to bring visual interest and warmth.

1 Smooth, light-coloured paving with minimal joints helps bring a calm, uncluttered feel.

2 The simple, elegant wooden structure with slatted roof allows light into the space while also blocking out excessive sunshine. You can find louvred roof systems with adjustable slats so that you can control how much shade they give. Running the length of the building, the horizontal lines overhead lead the eye to the planting at the far end of the terrace.

3 The lush green backdrop, made up of ground cover plants, shrubs and taller plants, brings texture, movement and coolness.

4 The low wooden seating and coffee tables are simple in design. The slats of the tables run in the same direction as the louvres overhead to give a considered look that is easy on the eye. The plain, cream coloured cushions are enhanced by the coordinating but textured cushions.

5 The large wooden planter, containing a tree and ground cover plants, is carefully positioned so that it is framed by the uprights and roofline of the veranda. The proportions ensure it holds its own against the tall, widely spaced uprights; a smaller container could easily look lost. Made of wood uprights held together by slim metal bands, the planter subtly echoes the materials used elsewhere.

6 The white, partially glazed vintage pot also adds texture and coordinates brilliantly with the textured cushioned. It's a subtle but clever pairing that adds a certain level of interest without distracting from the serenity of the whole scene.

7 The walls of the building are painted white which reflects the available light and ensures the veranda doesn't become overly dark.

8 Discreet wall lights signal the entrance to the building.

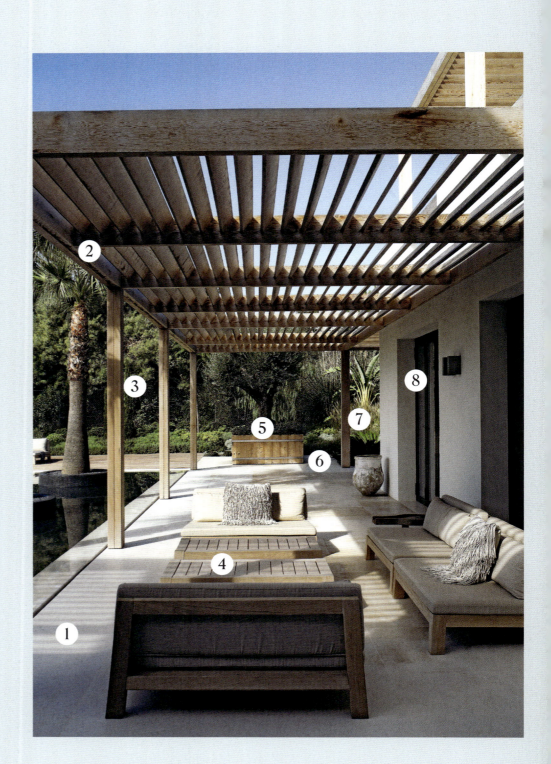

KEEP THINGS SIMPLE

Less is invariably more, so limit your use of different types of building materials. Leading garden designers recommend around between three to five different materials, although these may be used in different guises. For instance, you could have limestone paving and limestone chippings for gravel, or a wooden pergola with wooden deck beneath. Too many different materials and colours mean the eye is distracted, and the place will lack cohesion.

TAILOR YOUR COOKING AREA TO YOUR NEEDS

If you plan to cook outdoors, consider what and how often you want to cook before investing either too much or too little. If you simply want to cook pizzas as a family, then perhaps a simple pizza oven will suffice, or if you enjoy a barbeque then how many will you be cooking for at any one time? Do you prefer the taste imparted by charcoal or would a gas-fired barbecue be more convenient?

GET   THE   LOOK

PLAYFUL

PLAYFUL AREAS encompass everything from the fun, the funky and the slightly bonkers. This sort of styling benefits from creative thinking, innovation and the bold use of shapes, colours and materials. Styling in a playful way offers the opportunity to be highly inventive and pretty much throw out the rule book! That said, regardless of the look you wish to create, it's always good to bear in mind issues of comfort and practicality. Even spaces that are designed to appeal predominantly to our playful side should work well and be enjoyable places to hang out in. Scale and proportions can be interesting ways of creating drama, as can either a mix of colours or the repeat use of a particular colour palette. Plain, ornate, lively, or even challenging – as I said, anything goes.

Whether you choose to use plants in the design is a personal choice, however, they too can add a huge amount to the overall atmosphere. For instance, you may choose to combine a collection of plants with dramatic large leaves, or perhaps a mass planting of a single specimen, such as tall bamboos or grass.

The possibilities are endless, so why not be brave and let your imagination run wild. Some of us may worry that a crazy idea we have today may not pass the test of time, however, some designs can be so off the wall that they become timeless in themselves.

GET THE LOOK

GET THE LOOK

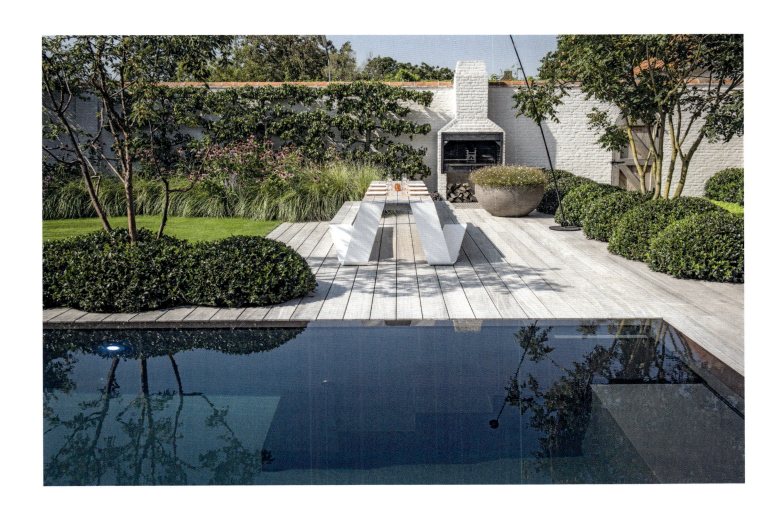

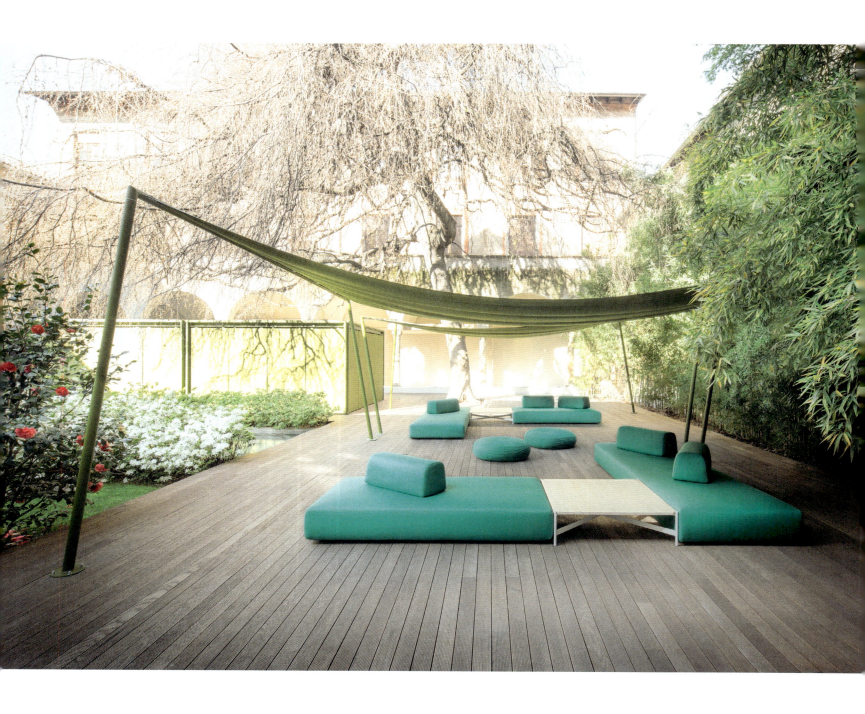

GET THE LOOK

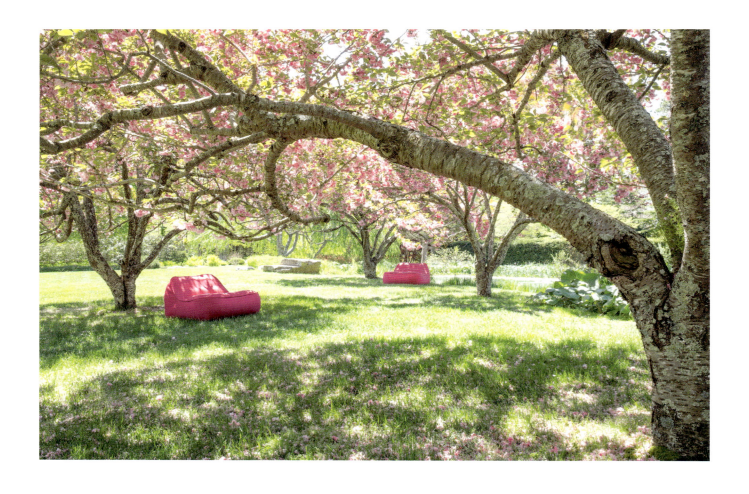

GET THE LOOK

TROPICAL ZONE

The scale of the planting, towering over the furniture, brings an unmistakable drama to this outdoor seating area. The unusual mix of turquoises, pinks, greys and the palest of greens work surprisingly well with the deep green foliage.

1 Extra-large planting containers arranged in a wide curve bring a sense of fun and weightiness to this outdoor space. They also ensure there's plenty of space for the root balls of the giant plants. The pots' various pastel colours in a matte finish work perfectly with those of the predominantly turquoise furniture, forming a cohesive and balanced look.

2 A mixture of large-leaved, exotic-looking plants in various sizes bring structure and drama to the setting.

3 A low coffee table on slim supports brings a touch of lightness to the rest of the substantial looking furniture and containers. The colour scheme – turquoises, pale greens and pinks – creates a peaceful, almost otherworldly, atmosphere that is distinct and memorable.

4 Outdoor rugs are a great way to add colour, cosiness and a feeling of connection to the interior of your home. Make sure they are specifically for use outside and can withstand rain and dirt.

5 The rich, dark green tops of these rounded, low white forms are a perfect match for the green leaves of the plantings scheme, bringing interest while ensuring a level of unity.

6 Large cushions provide seating and help give weight to the scene, drawing the eye down from the drama of the large plants.

7 The backdrop of a plain grey rendered wall helps emphasise the sculptural quality of the outsized plants and picks up the shadows cast by the leaves and stems.

SPLASH OF RED

The shapes, colours and understated design, along with a quirky little sculpture make this a place once seen never forgotten. While this is an assuredly pared-back design, everything is purposeful and carefully considered to create a dynamic and fun space to spend time in.

1 The bright red metal picnic table with integral seats immediately draws the eye and sets the tone for a quirky and fun atmosphere. It is both a useful piece of furniture that can be left out in all weather, but also a year-round sculptural form that enlivens the entire space.

2 A tall white semi-transparent screen at the back of the swimming pool adds a touch of theatricality. They are an interesting way to create a sense of enclosure and privacy without entirely blocking the view. Here the colour white ties with the seating to the right and keeps the palette simple and dramatic. Some screens can be lit up at night, which here would create a fun way to illuminate evening drinks around the pool or night-time swimming.

3 This simple rectangular pool, unadorned and noticeably clear of any distracting elements such as pool covers and other such paraphernalia, allows the other bolder elements of the furniture and sculpture to come to the fore.

4 The hard landscaping consists of plain wood decking, set horizontally across the space. Its streamline look sets a quiet scene in which the other elements can dominate.

5 A circular seating area with integral shade makes for an intimate dining area. Substantial in size, it holds its own against the red picnic table to the fore and the large rectangular sheet of water. Note that it is positioned to provide ease of movement around the pool.

6 A small, bright red sculpture in the form of a rabbit adds a note of whimsy and fun to the atmosphere.

WILD MEADOW

Not all playful areas are about bright colours and quirky shapes. This deck that floats above a froth of planting makes a fun and memorable experience for adults and children alike. It would make a magical destination for moments alone to daydream or a space of great privacy for sharing secrets with a friend.

1. The wooden walkway in slatted wood makes a sleek transition through the mass of planting to the lounging area. The light golden tones of the wood will silver over time.

2. The lounging area, in the same wood as the walkway, has sloping backrests on two opposite sides so that sitters can lean back while facing each other. The platform is raised off the ground so that it appears to float among the planting. Using slats rather than solid wood augments this feeling of lightness.

3. The backdrop of tall, airy golden oat grass (*Stipa gigantea*) glows in the sunlight and moves in the breeze, adding to a sense of joyfulness in the area.

4. The lounge area is centred on a single-stemmed tree, which brings dappled shade.

5. Simple cast concrete shapes form stepping stones from the walkway to the lounge area. Note the subtle change in height between the various elements. Level changes invariably add more dynamism to any design.

6. The soft ornamental grass and the veil-like forms of purple top (*Verbena bonariensis*) soften the rectilinearity of the wooden structures and give sitters a feeling of being enveloped by nature.

CREATE A NATURAL FLOW

To seamlessly link the house and the outside space, you might want to consider changing patio doors to bi-fold doors. Using the same flooring, such as stone or tiles in the interior and exterior spaces, also helps with a feeling of continuity. If you choose materials that are similar to those used inside, then it will feel like an extension of that space and both indoor and outdoor areas will appear larger.

TAKE THE UPKEEP INTO ACCOUNT

Consider how much time you have available for maintenance. Don't create an outdoor space that needs hours to maintain it if you don't have the time, energy or wherewithal to do so.

GET   THE   LOOK

EVERYDAY

THE AESTHETIC of this type of outdoor spaces can encompass many of the styles outlined above. What defines them is that they are spaces intended for everyday use. The best everyday spaces are unassuming, hardworking and comfortable with a welcoming atmosphere. Hard landscaping materials are often natural and hard-wearing. The best colours are those that are easy on the eye, just don't use too many of them. Some level of adornment is fine but preferably nothing too complicated or fussy. That said, everyday doesn't necessarily mean ordinary. It's mainly a question of the design lacking any form of pretension.

In terms of furniture and accessories, simple styles work well, and these can be dressed up with colourful accessories for particular occasions. Plants can make a great addition to an everyday aesthetic, particularly trees, shrubs and evergreens. It's an overall look and feel that we are aiming to achieve here and there are no strict guidelines you need to follow in order to achieve this. Just focus on a look that is effortless, easy-going, innately wholesome and congenial.

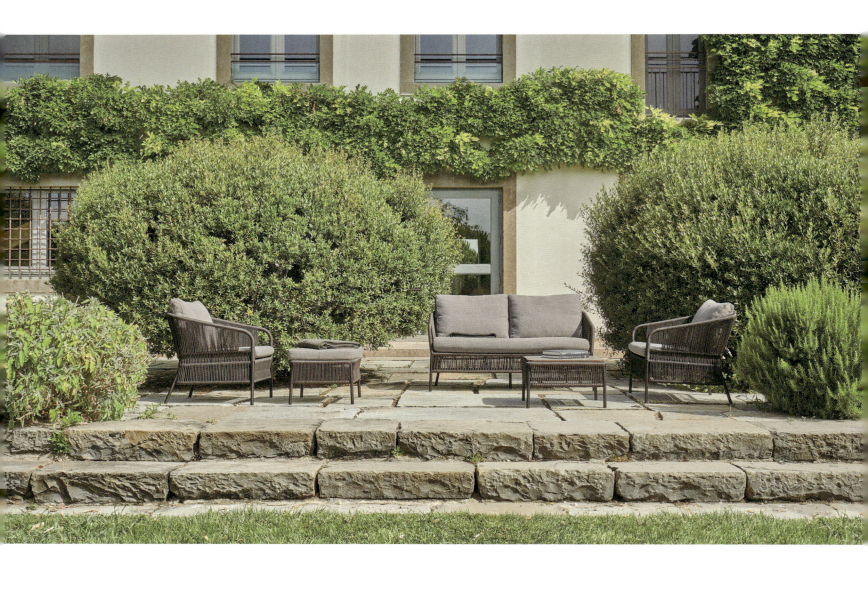

GET THE LOOK

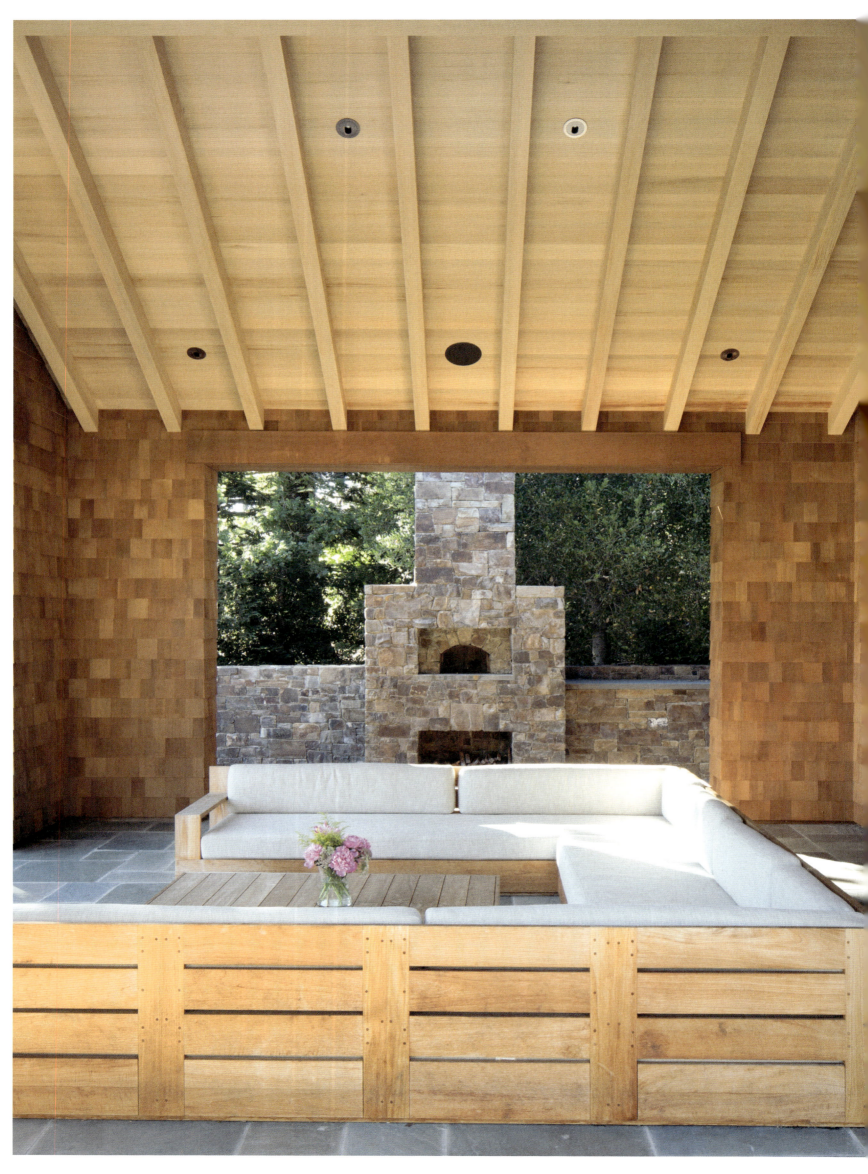

GET THE LOOK

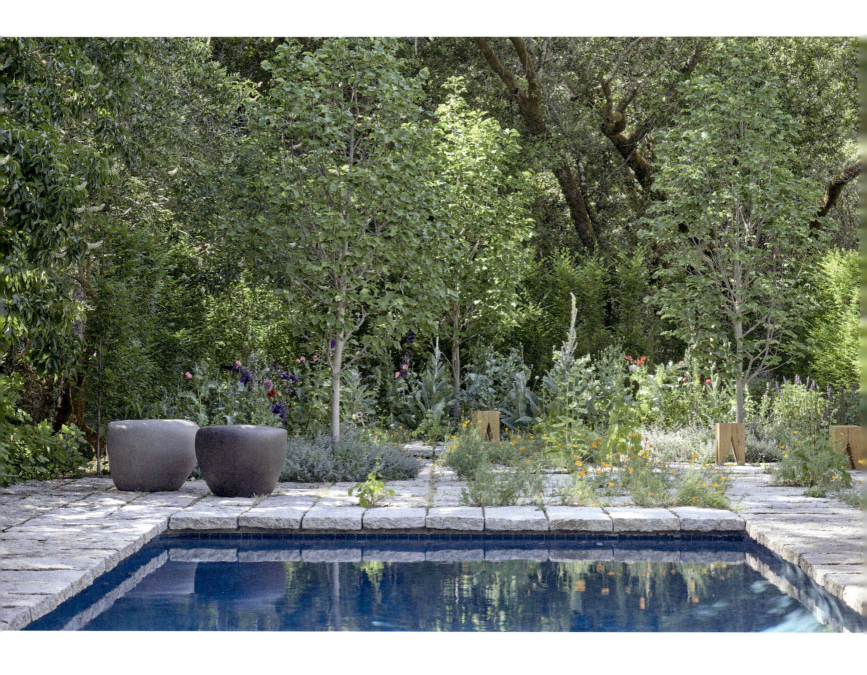

GET THE LOOK

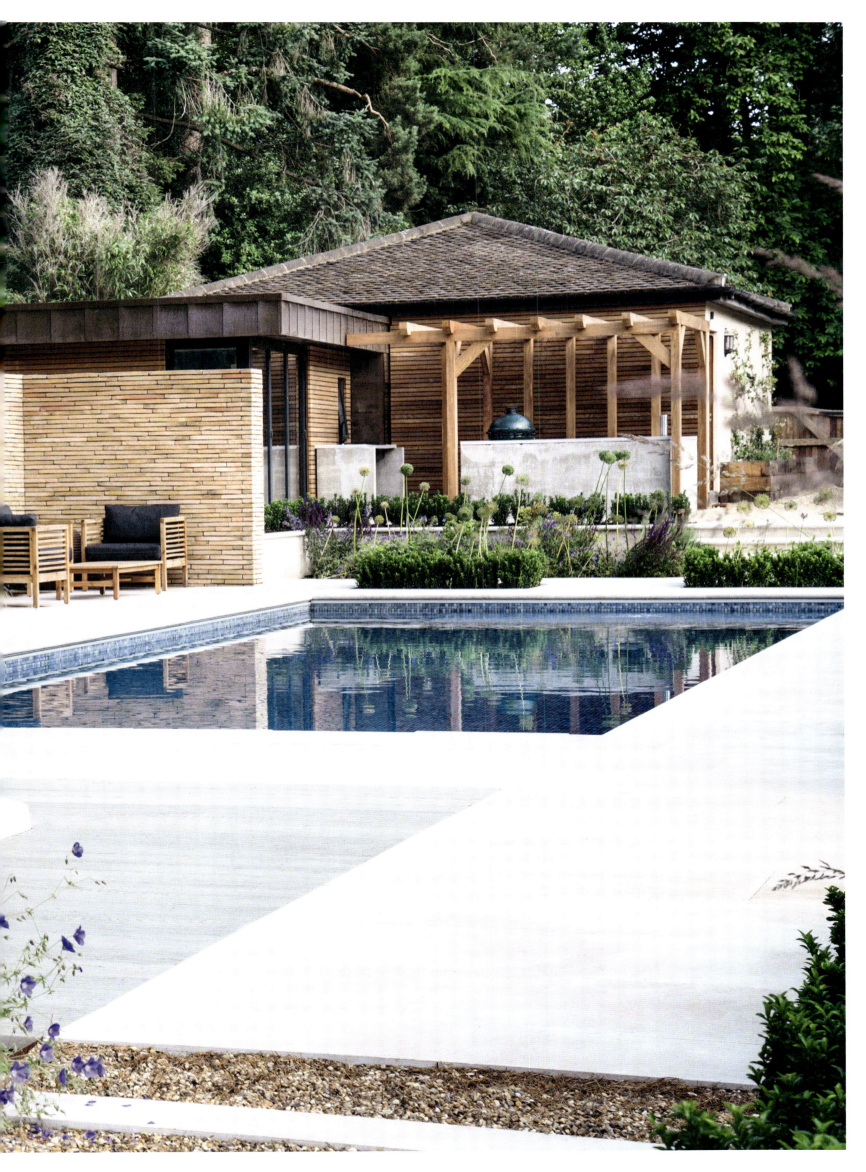

GET THE LOOK

GREEN CHOICE

This no-frills, wooden veranda provides a lovely cool spot next to the house. It is understated, inviting and comfortable – the perfect example of an everyday spot in which to relax alone or in company.

1. Climbing plants are a lovely way of adding texture and interest to simple structures. This one has a planting hole at the base of one of the supports and has formed thick swags that almost entirely cover the wooden fascia.

2. The light grey stone paving beneath the structure suits the natural, rustic nature of the structure. It provides a smooth surface on which to stand and place furniture, while setts paving blocks, which are more rounded and uneven, are used in the surrounding area.

3. The plain wooden boards form a backdrop to the veranda, adding warmth and character. Note the discreet hidden doorway to the right.

4. The green sofas bring the same feeling of comfort one expects to find inside a home. The colour perfectly matches the climber overhead, while the pale grey cushions coordinate with the paving.

5. A long wooden table is ideal for placing drinks and is low enough that it doesn't impede the view and feeling of openness. Keeping to a small number of different materials and colours makes sure the design hangs together well.

6. This standard lamp also underscores the feeling of being in a cosy interior space. Its wooden base and chocolate-coloured lampshade ensure everything remains nicely coordinated.

7. A dark grey planter containing flowers adds interest and colour to a shady corner and contributes to the atmosphere of the place being well tended and well loved.

SECRET GARDEN

This pretty dining area becomes the focal point of an unassuming garden space. Simply charming and irresistibly pretty, it's the ideal spot for afternoon tea and cakes.

1 A mix of climbers, shrubs and perennials plants, mainly in shades of green, are left to grow loosely helping to conjure up a romantic, secret-garden atmosphere.

2 The aged flint and red brick wall provides textural interest and a warmth to the seating area - both in terms of colour and reflected heat.

3 This charming garden parasol, with a wooden shaft, tassels and vintage-style green canopy, transforms an ordinary space into something quite magical.

4 The pale grey metal chairs and table, again in a vintage style, provide a charming place to sit beneath the parasol. Cushions, in co-ordinating colours, ensure the metal is more comfortable to sit on.

5 The tall trees in the background envelop the whole area with lush greenery and add to the feeling of being in an enchanting secret garden.

6 The simple square pavers provide a flat, stable and unobtrusive base for the furniture.

TRANQUIL HAVEN

What better way of extending time spent enjoying the weather than locating your outdoor kitchen right next to your swimming pool? Here, a u-shaped stone wall brings a sense of privacy and the simple palette of hard wearing materials is easy on the eye.

1 Swimming pools are great places to hang out in warm weather and if you build a kitchen and dining area alongside them, you can spend even more time outdoors.

2 Here, the outdoor sink and food preparation area has been positioned to one side of the kitchen, which ensures the pipework can be discreetly tucked out of sight and the central area can be devoted to the actual cooking.

3 A neatly manicured lawn, edged with shrubs in various shapes and sizes provides a calm green backdrop.

4 The stainless-steel unit containing the cooker and hob is set back from the pool. As those using the area will no doubt be scantily clad in swimwear, it's worth taking extra precautions to ensure there is adequate space around cooking facilities.

5 It's easy to overlook storage areas in outdoor spaces. This shelving unit is large enough to house useful items, including plates, bowls and glasses.

6 A stone wall surrounds the cooking area and makes a great place to perch a tray of drinks.

TAKE YOUR TIME

Many of us have budgetary or time constraints, so bear in mind that you don't necessarily have to create the entire outdoor space all at once. A good starting point is to have a scale plan of what will go where, that way you can build systematically in stages as and when time/money become available. As a general rule, it's a good idea to make sure the essentials such as electrics, water and drainage are in place and any digging work done first, as this will avoid mess and disturbance at a later date.

PRIORITISE SHADE

With much talk of climate change and temperatures set to rise in coming years, having a cool, comfortable outdoor space is becoming more important than ever. Whether it's a space to dine outdoors or a quiet spot where you can have a moment to yourself, there's always ways to make places cooler and more enjoyable to spend time in.

GET THE LOOK

MINIMALIST

SIMPLE, MINIMAL, PARED-BACK spaces are those where less is definitely more. They are generally characterised by the use of simple structures, forms and shapes with a distinct lack of adornment and fussiness. Simple spaces often belie how much thought and effort have gone into creating them. In many ways, the fewer objects you have in a space the more important each of them becomes so everything needs to be considered on merit. Anything that doesn't fit the overall picture often really stands out, with just one or two ill-considered items detracting from the overall mood.

Simple spaces tend to be restful on the eye and thus have serene atmospheres and if done really well, sometimes their restrained atmosphere can feel close to poetic. As well as there being a small number of items, there is frequently a stripped back colour scheme too. Often, neutral colours predominate although they aren't strictly necessary in order to achieve this particular look. That said, probably best to avoid too many colours as well as anything highly patterned. But an understated aesthetic doesn't have to be dull. Things such as texture, interesting shapes and bold forms, even shadow play on surfaces, can add layers of interest.

It should go without saying that furniture should be simple with clean lines. The same goes for planters and pots. Again, you can be bold, just make sure there is cohesion between the few elements you put in place.

You may or may not decide to include plants, but if you do make sure they aren't too fussy, and you don't have too much variety or a myriad of colours.

Clearing everything out so you begin with a blank canvas is helpful for whatever style you wish to create, but even more so when you're aiming for a pared-back look. As you introduce each item, be it furniture, lighting, sculpture, it's good to have a clear idea of the purpose they will serve. Remember the editing process is as much about what you include as what you choose not to include.

GET THE LOOK

GET THE LOOK

GET THE LOOK

GET THE LOOK

GET THE LOOK

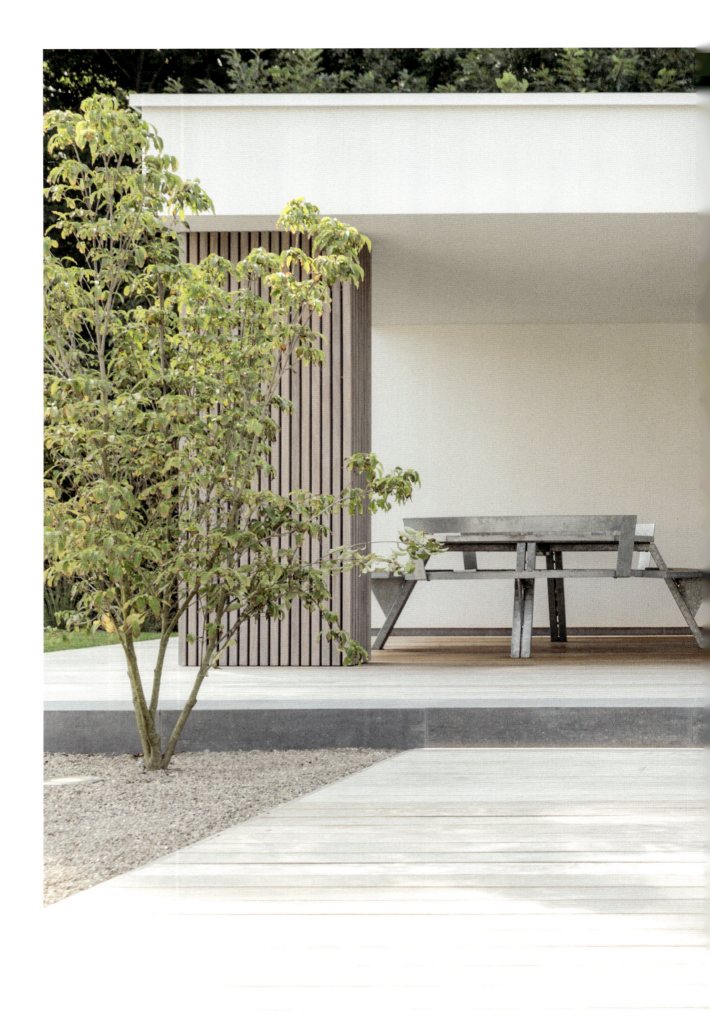

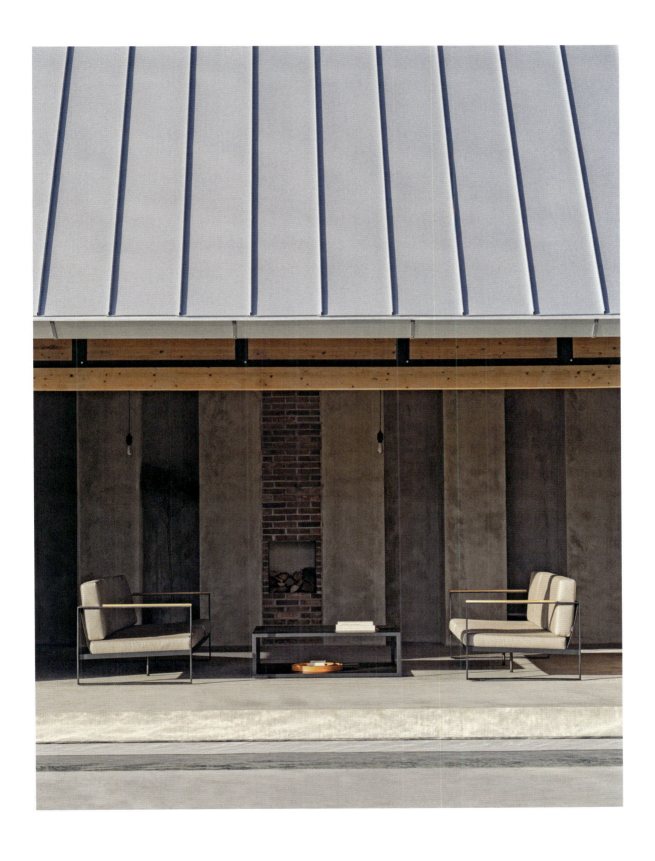

GET THE LOOK

GET THE LOOK

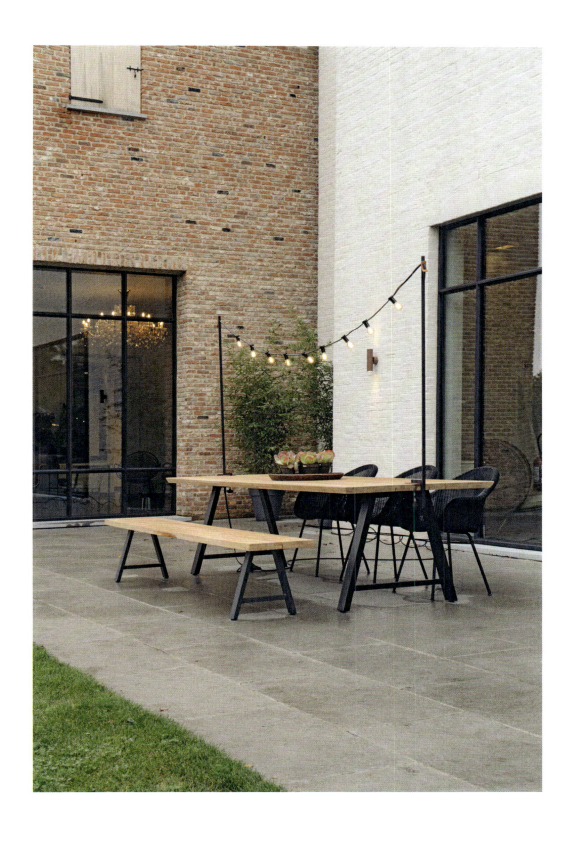

GREEN CANOPY

This simple structure made of slim pieces of metal discreetly attached to the building, is strong enough to support the weight of a substantial climbing plant. The whole look is understated, elegant and makes the perfect place to dine beneath the dappled light.

1 The walls of the building are painted white, which looks fresh and reflects available light so the area beneath the planting doesn't become overly dark.

2 Black-framed bi-fold doors, which fold neatly out of the way, allow the interior space to flow as seamlessly as possible into the outdoor dining area.

3 Gravel is a great material for covering large areas underfoot as it is relatively inexpensive, easy to use and comes in a range of colours. Note the paving before the entrance to the house, which helps prevent the gravel making its way indoors.

4 The wooden topped dining table and benches have slim metal legs that cleverly match the pergola structure. Benches tend to work better on gravel compared to chairs, as they feel more stable on the irregular surface.

5 The pergola is made of two L-shaped pieces of metal that are joined in several places across the top and fixed into the ground and to the side of the building. It has a feeling of lightness yet is incredibly strong so perfect for carrying the weight of climbing plants.

6 Deciduous climbing plants such as this vine are a great way of creating shade in the summer when the foliage is out and allowing light back into the area in winter as the leaves die back and fall off.

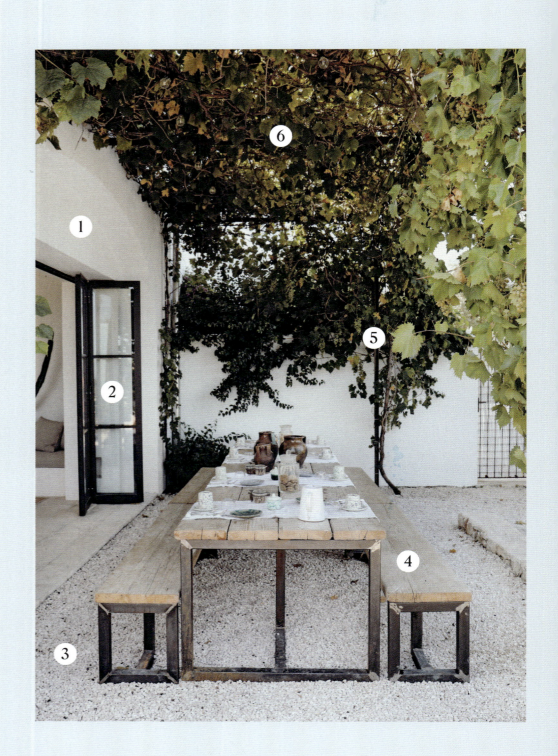

URBAN OASIS

This simple, elegant design relies heavily on the pared-back sculptural quality of the architecture and use of colour. The planting areas are integral to the hard landscaping and the only furniture are two loungers and a coffee table. A brilliant example of how few things it takes to create a strong sense of place.

1 Big-leaved exotic-looking plants spill over the edge of the wall, giving a feeling of exuberance.

2 The steps into the swimming pool are built in such a way that they feel like a continuation of those leading up the side of the building. Wide steps invariably create a feeling of generosity and expansiveness.

3 The semi-transparent backs of these low lounge chairs means that they feel light and airy. The white material subtly references the white curtains in the background.

4 A small table between the chairs has a curved top and textured finish so serves a useful purpose as well as adding interest to the space.

5 The pale turquoise colour of the pool works brilliantly with the pink-peach hard landscaping materials of the architecture.

6 Trees frame the seating area. Choosing those with multi-stem (rather than a single trunk) always makes a space more interesting and dynamic. The one at the lower level grows out of a purpose-built raised planting area, with lower ground cover plants at the base.

SIMPLE CURVES

A fine example of less is more. This simple but dramatic design features a flat hard surface that slopes down seamlessly to form a pool, while curved recliners and carefully positioned rocks provide beautiful and useful sculptural elements.

1 This swimming pool has what is termed a 'beach entry', which means that rather than having the more usual entry steps, it has a sloped edge so the water gets progressively deeper, mimicking a beach. The pool's turquoise base mirrors the colour of the sea in the distance.

2 The gradated sides of the pool extend out to form the lounging area. The timeless, pared-back aesthetic is also highly distinctive.

3 Two large rocks, which sit at the edge of the pool, add a natural, sculptural element to the area.

4 A mass of planting along the edge of the hard landscaping makes a connection with the wilder landscape beyond and contrasts with the sleekness of the hard landscaping elements.

5 Simple curved recliners in a neutral tone suit the pared-back aesthetic.

DO YOUR HOMEWORK

When employing a designer or contractor, it's worth seeing examples of their work and speaking to previous clients. Potentially, you may end up spending a considerable amount of money, therefore it's good to make sure you are confident in their abilities and their reliability. Ideally, get several recommendations and quotes so you can compare. Remember, the cheapest option is not necessarily the best one.

DON'T DIG TOO DEEP

Any excavation and moving around of soil will incur costs. If you wish to keep costs down, then try to design your outdoor space in such a way that these are avoided.

Credits

Text and Image Selection **Juliet Roberts**
Copy Editing **Léa Teuscher**
Book Design **Elise Castrodale**
Illustrations **Georgina Taylor**

www.lannoo.com
Sign up to our newsletter for updates on our latest publications on art, interior design, food & travel, photography and fashion, as well as exclusive offers and events.

If you have any questions or comments about the material in this book, please do not hesitate to contact our editorial team: art@lannoo.com

© Lannoo Publishers, Belgium, 2023
D/2023/45/17 - NUR: 425/648
ISBN 9789401488259
2nd print run